DevOps

From newbie to professional

Fast and simple guide to DevOps

Table of Contents

Introduction

It is good for you as a developer or as an IT professional to understand DevOps. This is a good way for one to ensure that there is a smooth running between members of the development team and the IT professionals of an organization. As a manager, you should set targets for your teams so that you can be in a position to measure their performance. The manager has the responsibility of making sure that they have the right data about the organization so as to make the best decisions. In this book, we will discuss the various DevOps operations. Program code samples will be used where necessary to ensure that there is ease of understanding.

Chapter 1- Making a Cultural Change in DevOps Teams

It is the desire of everyone to optimize the performance of their team, but this cannot be achieved just by talking. For the performance to be improved, we have to drive a cultural change among the DevOps teams. Metrics can be used for measuring the performance and the wellbeing of the team.

When there is the right data, the managers will easily and quickly make their decisions. The managers will also be in a position to see the actual outcome of the decisions that they make. This will make them create a more dynamic and happier working environment for their workers.

DevOps teams should monitor the following metrics to know their impact on the culture and performance of the team:

1. Use Time for Establishment of a Culture of High Performance.

    Time to respond is different for different team members. In the case of incident responders, even in cases in which they don't know the root cause of a problem, they will be quick to acknowledge and accept. Team members should be held accountable for their response time. This can be accomplished by setting targets and high expectations. In large IT companies, IT operations management tools are used for enforcing a target for the response time. With this, the managers are able to set up an incident response time window which will ensure that in any case that an incident happens, the next person who is in the line will be alerted. Tracking escalations will also help the managers in getting valuable data to understand their team members in depth.

2. Expectations should be managed with Escalations.

For companies in which the IT operations management tool is used, an escalation will be an expectation. This means that the responder was not in a position to acknowledge the incident in time or they lacked the tools or the skills for doing so. Escalation policies are very good in management of incidences, but your focus should be on driving the number of the escalations downwards. To track the performance of your team as a manager, you just have to track the number of incidents which have escalated over time. You should then make use of that data so as to check on whether there is need for the targets to be adjusted. Sometimes, an escalation can become part of a standard operating practice. If this become the case, you have to determine the types of alerts which should be escalated, and what the normal numbers should look like.

3. Use Raw Incident count to combat Alert fatigue.

When an organization grows, the incident counts also grow. However, when a particular team becomes more mature and efficient, the number of incidents per each responder should be reduced, or they become constant. When IT operations management tools have been implemented in an organization, they will assist the teams to lower their incident counts, since they will be in a position to factor out the low quality alerts. Common fixes will also be automated and runbooks created. With these, you will also be in a position to break down incident counts either by service or team, and the incidents will be put in context with the rest of the parts of the organization. They will be a way of ensuring that the team members are maximizing their time when attacking alerts that matter and whenever they are creating new features, and they will not be mired in the fatigues from alerts.

4. Measure Operational Readiness using Mean Time to resolution.

The time to resolution is the amount of time that a team takes to resolve a particular incident. This makes the highest standard in operational metrics. The time to resolution baseline is a variant in different organizations, and it normally depends on the complexity of the environment, the responsibilities of the organization, and the industry in which the organization operates in. When you track the time to response, the managers will be in a position to determine the norm mean time resolution, and to make sure that the development teams are in a position to withstand the challenges of a particular or major incident.

When the above metrics have been used in an organization, they will have the effect of combating possible downtime and increasing reliability. The teams will also become more focused on their work, number, and past performance.

However, the members also have to focus on the goals of the organization and know the reason why they are tracking the above metrics. The managers need not be over-focused on the past, but on the current situation and the future. Although they give information about the past performance of a team, one should not focus too much on them, but rather on how they can improve the performance of the various teams for the benefit of the future.

They should act as a means to an end of something negative in your organization, but avoid collecting more information about the organization than you need. This is because you won't be in a position to improve your team and business or organization. Your emphasis should be on subsequent action and with this, you will be in a position to drive a cultural change in your organization.

Chapter 2- Deployment with Capistrano, Thin, and nginx

Thin is a kind of a web server. Consider the nginx configuration file given below which is used to proxy requests to the Thin:

```
upstream thin {
  server 127.0.0.1:3000;
}
server {
  listen     80 default;
  server_name _;
  charset utf-8;
  rewrite  ^\/status(.*)$ $1 last;
  gzip  on;
  gzip_disable "MSIE [1-6]\.(?!.*SV1)";
  gzip_types        text/plain application/xml text/xml
text/css application/x-javascript application/xml+rss
text/javascript application/json;

  gzip_vary on;
  access_log
/var/www/graphs/shared/log/nginx_access.log;
  error_log
/var/www/graphs/shared/log/nginx_error.log;
  root  /var/www/thinkingingraphs/current/public;
  location / {
    proxy_pass http://thin;
  }
  error_page  404        /404.html;
  error_page  500 504 503 504 /500.html;
}
```

The following script can be used to start the thin server:

```
script
 export RACK_ENV=production
 export RUBY=ruby
 cd /var/www/graphs/current
 exec su -s /bin/sh vagrant -c '$RUBY -S bundle exec
thin           -p           3000           start           >>
/var/www/graphs/current/log/production.log 2>&1'

end script
```

When you have created a new version of the application, you can use the following Capistrano script for the purpose of starting and stopping the server:

```
namespace :deploy do
 task(:start) {}
 task(:stop) {}

 desc "Restart the Application"
 task :restart do
  sudo "stop graphs || echo 0"
  sudo "start graphs"
 end
end
```

However, there is a problem, though minor, which is associated with this approach. When the server is being restarted, the users will get a 504-response code as shown below:

$ bundle exec cap deploy

```
$ while true; do curl -w %{http_code}:%{time_total}
http://localhost/ -o /dev/null -s; printf "\n"; sleep 0.5;
done
```

```
200:0.076
200:0.074
200:0.095
504:0.003
200:0.696
```

To solve this, you should have more than one instances of the thin server in a state of execution. This means that in case you are restarting, the request can be sent to another instance. The following configuration script can help you in this:

```
chdir: /var/www/graphs/current
environment: production
address: 0.0.0.0
port: 3000
timeout: 30
log: log/thin.log
pid: tmp/pids/thin.pid
max_conns: 1013
max_persistent_conns: 100
require: []
wait: 30
servers: 4
daemonize: true
onebyone: true
```

Note that in the above script, we have used the property *"onebyone."* The purpose of this is to ensure that after restarting Thin, the instances will be taken one by one. This would also translate to the fact that the rest of the instances will be in a position to take care of the requests. In the above example, we have four servers on the different ports which we have specified, and these will handle the requests. The start script can then be changed to appear as follows:

```
script
  export RACK_ENV=production
  export RUBY=ruby
  cd /var/www/graphs/current
  exec su -s /bin/sh vagrant -c '$RUBY -S bundle exec thin -C /etc/thin/graphs.yml start >> /var/www/graphs/current/log/production.log 2>&1'

end script
```

The Capistrano script also has to be changed so that instead of having to stop and start the upstart script, we just call the *"thin script."* This is shown below:

```
namespace :deploy do
  task(:start) {}
  task(:stop) {}

  desc "Restart the Application"
  task :restart do
    run "cd #{current_path} && bundle exec thin restart -C /etc/thin/graphs.yml"

  end
end
```

The last part should involve configuring the nginx configuration file so that it can send requests to other configuration instances in any case in which the first attempt fails once it has been restarted. We have used the method "***proxy_next_upstream.***"This is shown below:


```
upstream thin {
  server          127.0.0.1:3000          max_fails=1
fail_timeout=20s;
  server 127.0.0.1:3001 max_fails=1 fail_timeout=20s;
  server          127.0.0.1:3004          max_fails=1
fail_timeout=20s;
}
server {
  listen    80 default;
  server_name _;
  charset utf-8;

  rewrite ^\/status(.*)$ $1 last;

  gzip on;
  gzip_disable "MSIE [1-6]\.(?!.*SV1)";
  gzip_types        text/plain application/xml text/xml
text/css application/x-javascript application/xml+rss
text/javascript application/json;


  gzip_vary on;

  access_log
/var/www/graphs/shared/log/nginx_access.log;
  error_log
/var/www/graphs/shared/log/nginx_error.log;

  root  /var/www/graphs/current/public;

  location / {
    proxy_pass http://thin;
```

```
    proxy_next_upstream    error    timeout    http_504
http_503;
  }

  error_page  404            /404.html;
  error_page  500 504 503 504 /500.html;
}
```

A change has also been made on the upstream definition to proxy requests to one of the running thin instances. There will be no downtime after deploying the application.

```
$ bundle exec cap deploy
$ while true; do curl -w %{http_code}:%{time_total}
http://localhost/ -o /dev/null -s; printf "\n"; sleep 0.5;
done

200:0.094
200:0.095
200:0.082
200:0.104
200:0.080
200:0.081
```

The problem will be that the upstart will have lost a handle from our Thin processes, and you have to know that there is no master process on which upstart can get a handle.

Chapter 3- ElasticSearch

ElasticSearch (ES)" is an open source, restful, and distributed search engine which is based on Lucene, and you can easily work with it. When developing your site, you should look for the best search solution for it. This is usually determined by your requirements.

ES offers the following functionalities:

1. RESTful- it can support the REST interface.

2. Distributed- the results of search are aggregated on multiple indices/shards.

3. Near real Time- it has the capability of supporting near real time updates.

4. Replication- replication of indices is supported.

5. Schema Less- it is document oriented. Automatic mapping types and JSON format are supported.

6. Versioning- different versions of the document are supported.

7. Index Aliasing- aliases for indices can be created.

8. Faceted Search- the navigation search functionality is supported.

9. Percolation- queries can be registered against an index, and the matching queries for a particular doc will be returned.

10. Fail over- it provides an inbuilt failover due to its distributed and replicated nature.

Installation of ElasticSearch

Begin by downloading the latest version of ES from its official site. If you are not aware of how to install it in your environment, consult the guides which are available online. The zipped file should be extracted in a destination folder and then moved to the installation folder. To begin the process in the foreground, execute the following command:

$ bin/elasticsearch

For the process to be started in the background, execute the following command:

$ bin/elasticsearch &

Executing ElastiSearch as a Service

Move to the GitHub repository, and then download the service wrapper. View the README file to know how to install it.

$ bin/service start/stop

Plugin Installation

We need to install the ES Head plugin. Begin by navigating to the installation directory as shown below:

$ bin/plugin -install mydirectory/elasticsearch-head

To browse for the plugin once you have installed it, open your browser and then type in the following URL:

http://localhost:9200/_plugin/head/

Configuration of ES server

For you to change the configuration settings for your server, navigate to the following directory:

$ vi config/elasticsearch.yml

You can then change the settings for ES for your environment. An example is changing the cluster name to what you need. Once you are done with making the changes, just restart the server for the changes to take effect. We now need to test our ES server. This can be done from the command line. An example of this is given below:

```
#Creating the Index
$ curl -XPUT 'http://localhost:9200/facebook/'

#Adding the document
$ curl -XPUT 'http://localhost:9200/facebook/post/1' -d '{
  "tweet" : {
    "user" : "john",
    "post_date" : "2012-11-14T16:12:18",
    "message" : "ElasticSearch is nice "
  }
}'

#Getting document by id
$ curl -XGET 'http://localhost:9200/facebook/post/1'

#Searching document
$ curl -XGET 'http://localhost:9200/facebook/post/_search?q=user:john'
```

For Java developers, you might need to establish a connection with the server.

Maven Integration

The elastic search Java API can be used together with maven dependency as shown below:

```
<dependency>
<groupId>org.elasticsearch</groupId>
<artifactId>elasticsearch</artifactId>
<version>0.20.5</version>
</dependency>
```

The Java API

To use this in this case, you have to follow the following steps:

- Create the client.
- Create the index, and set mappings and settings for the document type.
- The documents should then be added to the index.
- Get the document

This is shown below:

```
//Creating the Client

Settings settings =
ImmutableSettings.settingsBuilder().put("cluster.name", "mytestsearch").build();

TransportClient tClient = new
TransportClient(settings);
```

```
tClient = transportClient.addTransportAddress(new
InetSocketTransportAddress("localhost", 9300));

return (Client) tClient;
```

//Creating the Index and setting the settings and the mappings

```
CreateIndexRequestBuilder cIRequestBuilder =
client.admin().indices().prepareCreate(indName);

cIRequestBuilder.execute().actionGet();
```

```
//Adding the documents
IndexRequestBuilder iRBuilder =
client().prepareIndex(indName, documentType,
documentId);
```

```
//building a json object
XContentBuilder contBuilder =
jsonBuilder().startObject().prettyPrint();
contBuilder.field("name", "john");
contBuilder.stopObject();
iRBuilder.setSource(contBuilder);
IndexResponse response = iRBuilder
.execute().actionGet();
```

```
//Getting the document
GetRequestBuilder gRBuilder =
client().prepareGet(indName, type, id);
```

```
gRBuilder.setFields(new String[]{"name"});
GetResponse response =
gRBuilder.execute().actionGet();
String name =
response.field("name").getValue().toString();
```

That is it, it is done.

Chapter 4- Analyzing Text for Content Enrichment

Text search is very powerful, like text analysis. Lucene is an open source library for retrieving information. In ES, the inbuilt text analysis capabilities of Lucene are used to enrich the search content. The various divisions of text analysis are filters tokenizers and analyzers.

Update Analysis Settings

With ES, the update of mapping and index setting can be done dynamically. For the index setting to be updated from the Java API client, the following can be done:

```
Settings                    settings                =
settingsBuilder().loadFromSource(jsonBuilder()
          .startObject()
              //Adding the analyzer settings
              .startObject("analysis")
                 .startObject("filter")

.startObject("test_filter_stopwords_en")
                  .field("type", "stop")
                  .field("stopwords_path",
"stopwords/stop_en")

                  .endObject()

.startObject("test_filter_snowball_en")
                  .field("type", "snowball")
                  .field("language", "English")
                .endObject()

.startObject("test_filter_worddelimiter_en")
                  .field("type", "word_delimiter")
```

```java
                    .field("protected_words_path",
"worddelimiters/protectedwords_en")
                    .field("type_table_path",
"typetable")
                .endObject()

.startObject("test_filter_synonyms_en")
                    .field("type", "synonym")
                    .field("synonyms_path",
"synonyms/synonyms_en")

                    .field("ignore_case", true)
                    .field("expand", true)
                .endObject()
                .startObject("test_filter_ngram")
                    .field("type", "edgeNGram")
                    .field("min_gram", 2)
                    .field("max_gram", 30)
                .endObject()
            .endObject()
            .startObject("analyzer")
                .startObject("test_analyzer")
                    .field("type", "custom")
                    .field("tokenizer", "whitespace")
                    .field("filter",                    new
String[]{"lowercase",

"test_filter_worddelimiter_en",

"test_filter_stopwords_en",

"test_filter_synonyms_en",

"test_filter_snowball_en"})
                    .field("char_filter", "html_strip")
                .endObject()
            .endObject()
        .endObject()
    .endObject().string()).build();
```

**CreateIndexRequestBuilder cIRequestBuilder =
client.admin().indices().prepareCreate(indName);**

cIRequestBuilder.setSettings(settings);

The index and the settings can also be set in the configuration file. What about the case of synonyms? These are the names having the same meaning. In Synonym Expansion, we take the variants of a word and then they are assigned to the search engine during the query or indexing time. For the synonym filter to be added to the index settings, do the following:

```
.startObject("test_filter_synonyms_en")
   .field("type", "synonym")
        .field("synonyms_path",
"synonyms/synonyms_en")
        .field("ignore_case", true)
        .field("expand", true)
.endObject()
```

The synonym can be added in either Slor or WordNet format. An example for this is given below:

 # If expand==true, "ipod, i-pod, i pod" is similar to the explicit mapping:

ipod, i-pod, i pod => ipod, i-pod, i pod
 # If expand==false, "ipod, i-pod, i pod" is similar to the explicit mapping:

ipod, i-pod, i pod => ipod

Stemming

This refers to the ability for one to include the variations for a word. A good example of this is a noun word. In this case, quantified methods are used for the rules of the grammar so as to add word stems and then rank them based on the degree of Augaration from your root word. For the stemming filter to be added to the index for settings, the following can be done:

```
.startObject("test_filter_snowball_en")
   .field("type", "snowball")
   .field("language", "English")
.endObject()
```

The programs for stemming are always referred to as stemming algorithms. The Lucene analysis can either be dictionary or algorithm based.

Stop words

This represents the set of words which you do not want your user to query or index upon. For a stop word filter to be added to the settings, do the following:

```
.startObject("test_filter_stopwords_en")
    .field("type", "stop")
    .field("stopwords_path", "stopwords/stop_en")
.endObject()
```

Word Delimiter

With this, one finds it easy for them to split a particular word into a set of sub words. This is usually for the purpose of further processing of the sub words. For a word delimiter to be added to the settings, do the following:

```
.startObject("test_filter_worddelimiter_en")
  .field("type", "word_delimiter")
      .field("protected_words_path",
"worddelimiters/protectedwords_en")

      .field("type_table_path", "typetable")
.endObject()
```

The process of splitting the words is based on a non alphanumeric nature, intra word delimiters, and case transitions. When you have a list of protected words, you will be in a position to protect some words which are relevant to your business, and they will not be delimited in the process.

N-grams

This is just a continuous sequence of n letters representing a certain sequence of text. For an edge ngram filter to be added to the settings, do the following:

```
.startObject("test_filter_ngram")
        .field("type", "edgeNGram")
        .field("min_gram", 2)
        .field("max_gram", 30)
.endObject()
```

Depending on your configuration, the text that you provide as the input will be broken down into a number of tokens of the length that you configure above. Note that this will be done during the time of indexing. The returned result will be based on the matching ngram tokens and the proximity.

Char Filter

The HTML content for most websites is indexable. In most sites, it is not desirable for one to index and query on standard html text. With the ES, the html tags can be filtered. Consider the example given below showing how this can be done:

```
.startObject("analyzer")
   .startObject("test_analyzer")
               .field("type", "custom")
               .field("tokenizer", "whitespace")
               .field("filter",                    new
String[]{"lowercase",
"test_filter_worddelimiter_en",
"test_filter_stopwords_en",
"test_filter_synonyms_en",
"test_filter_snowball_en"})

               .field("char_filter", "html_strip")
   .endObject()
.endObject()
```

There are also other filters which can help you in enriching your contents search in the best way, depending on the requirements of the end user and the business data.

Chapter 5- Searchable Documents

Asciidoctor is a Ruby processor used for conversion of AsciiDoc source files and strings into DocBook 4.5, HTML5, and other formats. In this chapter, we will show you how you can use the **Elasticsearch** on *AsciiDoc* documents so as to make them searchable using their header information or by the content. The following are the dependencies which are needed:

```
<dependencies>
            <dependency>
            <groupId>myId</groupId>
            <artifactId>myId</artifactId>
            <version>4.11</version>
            <scope>test</scope>
      </dependency>
      <dependency>

      <groupId>com.googlecode.lambdaj</groupId>
>
            <artifactId>myId</artifactId>
            <version>2.3.3</version>
      </dependency>
      <dependency>

      <groupId>org.elasticsearch</groupId>
            <artifactId>elasticsearch</artifactId>
            <version>0.90.1</version>
      </dependency>
      <dependency>
            <groupId>org.asciidoctor</groupId>
            <artifactId>asciidoctor-java-
integration</artifactId>
            <version>0.1.3</version>
      </dependency>
```

</dependencies>

The library *"Lambdaj"* is used for conversion of *AsciiDoc* files to JSON documents. You can then launch an instance of the ES engine and in this case, it has to be an embedded instance. This can be done by executing the following command:

node = nodeBuilder().local(true).node();

The next step should involving parsing of the *AsciiDoc* document header. Its contents should be read and then converted into a JSON format.

Below is an example of a JSON document which has been stored in ES:

```
{
  "title":"Asciidoctor Maven plugin 0.1.2 released!",
  "authors":[
    {
      "author":"Alex John",
      "email":"email@mail.com"
    }
  ],
  "version":null,
  "content":"=   Asciidoctor   Maven   plugin   0.1.2
released!.....",
  "tags":[
    "release",
    "plugin"
  ]
}
```

To convert the AsciiDoc into a JSON format, we have to use the class *"XContentBuilder."* This is provided by the **Elasticsearch** *Java API,* which is used for creation of JSON documents in a programming manner. This is shown below:

```
package com.lordofthejars.asciidoctor;
import org.asciidoctor.DocumentHeader;
import java.io.File;
import java.io.FileInputStream;
import static
org.elasticsearch.common.xcontent.XContentFactory
.*;

import java.io.FileNotFoundException;
import java.util.List;
import
org.elasticsearch.common.xcontent.XContentBuilder
;
import org.asciidoctor.Asciidoctor;
import java.io.IOException;
import org.asciidoctor.Author;
import ch.lambdaj.function.convert.Converter;
import org.asciidoctor.internal.IOUtils;


public class AsciidFJConverter implements
Converter<File, XContentBuilder> {

        private Asciidoctor asdoctor;

        public AsciidFJConverter () {
                this.asdoctor =
Asciidoctor.Factory.create();
        }

        public XContentBuilder convert(File
asdoctor) {
```

```java
                DocumentHeader docHeader =
this.asdoctor.readDocumentHeader(asdoctor);

                XContentBuilder jContent = null;
                try {
                        jContent = jBuilder()
                                .startObject()
                                .field("title",
documentHeader.getDocumentTitle())

.startArray("authors");

                                        Author
mnAuthor = documentHeader.getAuthor();


    jContent.startObject()

    .field("author", mnAuthor.getFullName())

    .field("email", mnAuthor.getEmail())

    .endObject();

                                List<Author>
authors = docHeader.getAuthors();

                                for (Author
author : authors) {

    jsonContent.startObject()

    .field("author", author.getFullName())

    .field("email", author.getEmail())

    .endObject();
                                }
```

```java
                    jContent.endArray()

        .field("version",
dHeader.getRevisionInfo().getNumber())


        .field("content", readContent(asdoctor))


        .array("tags",
parseTags((String)documentHeader.getAttributes().g
et("tags")))

                            .endObject();
            } catch (IOException e) {
                    throw                    new
IllegalArgumentException(e);
                    }

            return jContent;
        }

        private String[] parseTags(String tags) {
                tags = tags.substring(1, tags.length()-
1);
                return tags.split(", ");
        }

        private  String  readContent(File  content)
throws FileNotFoundException {

                return              IOUtils.readFull(new
FileInputStream(content));
        }

}
```

That is it. For us to build the JSON document, we have to call the method *"startObject"* so as to start a new object, the method *"field"* for addition of new fields, and the method *"startArray"* for starting a new array. The builder will then be used for rendering the equivalent object in the JSON format. The method *"readDocumentHeader"* from the class *"Asciidoctor"* is also used for returning the header attributes from the file *"AsciiDoc"* without the need to read and render the whole document. The final step should involve setting the content field with all of the document content.

At this point, we should be ready to begin the process of indexing our documents. The code for the example is given below:

```
import static ch.lambdaj.Lambda.convert;
//....
private void populateData(Client client) throws IOException {
        List<File> asdocFiles = new ArrayList<File>() {{
                add(new File("target/test-classes/java_release.adoc"));

                add(new File("target/test-classes/maven_release.adoc"));

        }};

        List<XContentBuilder> jDocuments = convertAsciidoctorFilesToJson(asdocFiles);


        for (int j=0; j < jDocuments.size(); j++) {
                client.prepareIndex("docs", "asciidoctor", Integer.toString(j)).setSource(jsonDocuments.get(j)).execute().actionGet();
```

```
        }

        client.admin().indices().refresh(new
RefreshRequest("docs")).actionGet();

}

private                      List<XContentBuilder>
conAsDocFilesToJson(List<File> asciidoctorFiles) {

                return    convert(asdocFiles,    new
AsciidoctorFileJsonConverter());

}
```

That is how we can do it. Note that in the first part of our application shown above, we have converted all of our *AsciiDoc* files into instances of *XContentBuilder* by use of the previous converter class and the *"convert"* method of the project Lambdaj.

Now that we are done with the above, we can begin to query the ES so as to retrieve data from the AsciiDoc documents. This is shown below:

```
SearchResponse response =
client.prepareSearch().execute().actionGet();
```

We want to search for all of the documents which have been written by the author *"Alex John."* I n our case, we have a single document written by this author. The following code can be used for this purpose:

```
import static
org.elasticsearch.index.query.QueryBuilders.
matchQuery;
    //....
```

```
QueryBuilder matchQuery = matchQuery("author",
"Alex John");
```

```
QueryBuilder matchQuery = matchQuery("author", "
Alex John ");
```

The above code can give us the result. What we have done is that we have searched from the field for "*author*" and we are looking for the string named "*Alex John.*" This is what will give us the result. When there are complexities or similarities in the names, the ES is very efficient in this, and it knows what to do. That is how powerful it is.

There are multiple queries which we can use. What about a scenario in which you need all the documents written by Alex but not John? This can be achieved as follows:

```
import static
org.elasticsearch.index.query.QueryBuilders.fieldQuery;
```

```
//...
•
```

```
QueryBuilder  matchQuery  =  fieldQuery("author",
"+Alex -John");
```

In this case, you will get no result since no document will be found according to the specified criteria. In the above case, we have a field query other than a term query. The words have been included and excluded by use the symbols + and − respectively.

If you need to display all the documents whose title have the word *"releases,"* the following query can be used:

import
static org.elasticsearch.index.query.QueryBuilders.
matchQuery;

//....

QueryBuilder matchQuery = matchQuery("title", "released");

To find the document which is about the release version "0.1.2," use the query given below:

QueryBuilder matchQuery = matchQuery("content", "0.1.2");

Note that in our case, only one document is talking about that release since the other one is talking about version "0.1.3."

It is now time for us to send the query to our ES database. This can be done by use of the method *"prepareSearch."* This is shown below:

```
    .setTypes("asciidoctor")
    .setQuery(matchQuery)
    .execute()
     .actionGet();

SearchHits hits = response.getHits();

 for (SearchHit searchHit : hits) {
    System.out.println(searchHit.getSource().
 get("content"));
 }
```

Remember that in this case, the AsciiDoc will be printed via the console, but for you to render the document in the required format, you have to use the method *"asciidoctor.render(String content, Options options)."*

You are now aware of how you can index your documents by use of the ES. You are also in a position to use the project **"Asciidoctor-java-integration project"** so as to get some important information from the AsciiDoc files. Note that there are multiple queries which can be used in ES, but this book gives you an insight into some of them. You should be aware of the importance of the AsciiDoc format so as to write your documents. You can choose to build your search engine for your documentation and much effort will not be required for you to do this.

Chapter 6- Working with tc

When it comes to identification of problems associated with performance, there are multiple ways how this can be done. However, nearly all of these methods rely on iterative improvement. You should begin by setting up a performance target such as a latency limit on a page load or the number of concurrent connections that can be handled. A test should then be put up or implemented, and this will tell you whether or not you are meeting that target. A bench or the jmeter can be used for loading testing the system. The set up can then be tuned and optimized so that the target is met.

Sometimes, the Internet connection can be poor, resulting to a very slow network and especially for people residing in rural areas. Replicating slow connections on a phone can also be a bit time consuming. You only need a command for slowing down a regular network connection and the problem will be replicated, but not much hassle should be involved.

Use of tc to replicate a slow network

Tc is a Linux command line program which stands for *"Traffic Control."* With it, you can take a regular network interface and then introduce an additional latency or perform a reduction on the bandwidth which is available. If you are in need of knowing the full details of this tool, just take a view of its manual. In this chapter, we will guide you on how to add some rules to your machine so as to simulate some simple problems. In tc, the individual rules will be referred to as *Queuing Discipline* or *qdisc*.

If you are in need of viewing all of the qdisc rules, you can make use of the *"ls"* command. Below is an example of a lo interface:

tc -s qdisc ls dev lo

You should know how to limit the available bandwidth. You should begin by substituting a new queuing discipline for the loopback device. This is shown below:

tc qdisc add dev lo handle 1: root htb

The rate command can be used for adding a qdisc that will limit lo to only 100kbps. This is shown in the command given below:

tc class add dev lo parent 1: classid 1:11 htb rate 100kbps

For the sake of understanding the above command, it can be broken down into various parts. The class "*add*" will inform tc that we are adding a new class, and it will be a tree of queuing problems. The property "*dev lo*" will specify that we are making use of a loopback interface. The classes used here can be used for making a tree and then be identified, since tc was developed to allow for some complex filters to be built up. The htb is a method which will control an outbound traffic on a particular network device. The property "*rate 100kbps*" is responsible for setting the maximum rate that we need our traffic to go at. You should be clear on this point since the tc is capable of accepting both 100kbps and 100kBps, and this will depend on whether you are in need of kilobytes or kilobits.

Latency

We can make use the command *"delay"* so as to add a qdisc which will introduce 300ms of lag to lo. This is shown in the command given below:

tc qdisc add dev lo parent 1:11 netem delay 300ms

Once you break up the above command, you will notice that what you are adding is a qdisc but not a command. The loopback is being used as the device, so that is why we have used *"dev lo."* We previously specified the parent in the tree, and we have used the parent *"1:11."* The *"classid 1:11"* has been used for setting up the class identifier. With *"delay 300ms,"* the tc will be notified to make an addition of 300ms of lag.

Limiting Ports

In some cases, there may be other connections talking over your similar network device, meaning that all of these will be limited to 3G. The speed test will then not be a faster one. Our aim is to come with a filter which we will add and apply it to the port 8080 only. A filter acts as a restriction so as to apply to the qdisc to specific or certain conditions only. This is shown in the command given below:

tc filter add dev lo protocol ip prio 1 u32 match ip dport 8080 0xffff flowid 1:11

To add the fiter, we have used the property *"filter add"* and then the property *"dev lo"* has been used to specify the device to which it applies. The property *"protocol ip"* is responsible for specifying the ip protocol as it has been said in the tin. The property *"prio 1"* has been used for specifying the priority of the filter. With the priorities set up, you will be in a position to know the class to which you will assign any additional bandwidth in case it is available and to know whether the rules which you have applied have been followed. *u32* is the type of filter rule which we are making use of. *match ip dport 8080* will tell the tc to look up for the port 8080 as the destination of our incoming requests. With the bitmask *0xffff,* the u32 filter will be forced to look at the whole of the header. In case you have multiple qdiscs, tc will have to know the rule which is to be used, so *flowid 1:11* will specify the identifier which we used before our parent class. Those are the full details about the command, and my hope is that you are now aware of each and every aspect associated with it.

Once you are done with the process of benchmarking, you will need to return to normal. You may need to do away or delete the restrictions which you have imposed on the "lo" interface. This can be done by executing the command given below:

tc qdisc del dev lo root

With the approach we have discussed above, one can easily test whether or not a change that they have made to their system is really working or not. Less time will be consumed as compared to replication on the real devices. Once you are sure that the optimizations which you have made have really worked effectively, you can then test it on a real device. The changes made should be well validated not only in the lab but also in the wild. There is a difference between the changes that you have made and a real slow network.

Chapter 7- Couchbase Cluster by use of Docker Compose

With Couchbase 4.0, you are provided with lots of features which can allow you to develop with agility and operate at any scale that you need. The following are some of the features which can allow you to operate at the scale that you need:

- Elastic Scalability
- Always Available
- High Performance consistently
- Easy and Powerful Administration
- Security, Enterprise level

Creation of Couchbase Nodes

The Docker Compose file given below can easily be used for creation of a Couchbase cluster:

```
couchbase1:
  image: couchbase/server
  volumes:
   - ~/couchbase/node1:/opt/couchbase/var
couchbase2:
  image: couchbase/server
  volumes:
   - ~/couchbase/node2:/opt/couchbase/var
couchbase3:
  image: couchbase/server
  volumes:
   - ~/couchbase/node3:/opt/couchbase/var
  ports:
   - 8091:8091
   - 8092:8092
   - 8093:8093
   - 11210:11210
```

In the above file, we have three service definitions for only three couchbase nodes. The ports for the Admin have only been exposed to one node, since the others will communicate with each other via IP addresses which have been internally assigned by the Docker.

Begin by creating the three directories. You can then use "*docker-compose.yml*" to start only three couchbase nodes. This is shown below:

```
> docker-compose up -d
Pulling couchbase1 (couchbase/server:latest)...
latest: Pulling from couchbase/server
70618b6e8070: Pull complete
05820377a11a: Pull complete
8de88a91bde5: Pull complete
61994089e28e: Pull complete
bc191c81777b: Pull complete
939d0c2514c9: Pull complete
fa75256f7885: Pull complete
7bc9fb79dd30: Pull complete
e4c99c5f6106: Pull complete
307ac999aa30: Pull complete
13eeb78ce9ab: Pull complete
c4180973b487: Pull complete
6e0c54ca80e7: Pull complete
c6d69cc874d9: Pull complete
31485a5bae7a: Pull complete
31c8df734d6b: Pull complete
Digest:
sha256:0e983929897ae9bd396533ff7875f30047290c
6acf164a66c967ca8884507381
Status: Downloaded ne
wer image for couchbase/server:latest
Creating couchbasecluster_couchbase1_1
Creating couchbasecluster_couchbase3_1
Creating couchbasecluster_couchbase2_1
```

The command should be issued on a Docker Machine. The next step should involve checking the status of your nodes. The necessary commands together with their output are shown below:

```
> docker ps
```

There is the command. It should give the details about the nodes. A sample output from the command is given below:

```
CONTAINER ID     IMAGE          COMMAND
07ff4f1823a4     couchbase/server  "/entpoint.sh
couch"
18f7bf07134a     couchbase/server  "/entpoint.sh
couch"
4db3e1280776     couchbase/server  "/entpoint.sh
couch"
```

The Docker Dompose can also be used for showing the status as shown below:

> docker-compose ps

It will give you the status of the nodes.
You can then check the logs for the nodes as shown below:

> docker-compose logs
Attaching   to   couchbasecluster_couchbase2_1,
couchbasecluster_couchbase3_1,
couchbasecluster_couchbase1_1

couchbase2_1 | Starting Couchbase Server -- Web UI available at http://<ip>:8091

couchbase3_1 | Starting Couchbase Server -- Web UI available at http://<ip>:8091

couchbase1_1 | Starting Couchbase Server -- Web UI available at http://<ip>:8091

The above is the command and its output.

Configuration of the Couchbase Cluster

The nodes should now be configured so that they can become part of the cluster. The following steps are necessary:

1. Begin by finding the IP address of your Docker machine:

   >> docker-machine ip default

2. Open the Admin Console of the couchbase via the URL *http://<DOCKER_MACHINE_IP:8091*. You will get an output similar to the one given below:

Click on the "*Setup*" button.

3. Docker assigns an internal IP address to each container, and all containers which are being executed on the same host can view the IP address of a particular container. Our aim is to use these internal IP addresses so as to add the new nodes to a cluster. Begin by identifying the IP address of the first container as shown below:

> docker inspect --format '{{ .NetworkSettings.IPAddress }}' couchbasecluster_couchbase3_1

The IP address should then be used for changing the field for the host name.

4. You can then click on the "*Next*" button. If possible, adjust the RAM.

5. Identify your best bucket to be installed and then click on "*Next.*"

6. Change the value for Per Node RAM Quota from 400 to 100. This is necessary as the other nodes are to be added later.

7. Click on Next, accept the T&C and then click on Next.

8. Provide the password for it, and this will be used for adding more nodes to the cluster.

Add More Couchbase Nodes

There are other two nodes which we used Docker Compose to create. We need to add them to the cluster. The following steps are necessary:

1. Click on the "Server Nodes" so as to have a default view as shown below:

2. Look for the IP address for one of your remaining nodes as shown below:

docker   inspect   --format   '{{ .NetworkSettings.IPAddress   }}' couchbasecluster_couchbase1_1

3. Click on the "*Add Server,*" and then specify the IP address. You can then click on "*Add Server.*"

4. Use the server name to repeat our previous two steps.

Chapter 8- Multiple Tomcat Instances

There are different stages in the development of a real software application. In each of these stages, one might need to have different environments in which to deploy the application. For one to do versioning, configurations, testing, and bug fixing, different environments are needed. When it comes to shared servers and performing upgrades, this can bring about challenges.

The easiest way that one can set up multiple instances of Tomcat is to perform a duplication of the entire Tomcat folder and then change some of the configurations. However, when this is done, it becomes hard to maintain, spin up new instances, and to perform an upgrade. However, we will do this in a way which is very flexible and easy way in which we will duplicate only a few things, and then maintain a shared base folder for all of our instances.

Installation

Once you have the download folder, unzip it in a directory of your choice. You can use a parent folder to do this. We need to create a link leading to the unzipped folder other than using the unzipped folder. This is shown below:

mydirectory:tomcat mydirectory$ pwd
/usr/local/files/java/tomcat
mydirectory:tomcat mydirectory$ ln -s apache-tomcat-7.0.64/ current

mydirectory:tomcat mydirectory$ ls
total 8
drwxr-xr-x   4 mydirectory admin   136B Aug 13 04:30 .
drwxr-xr-x@ 26 mydirectory admin   884B Aug 13 04:30 ..
drwxr-xr-x   13 mydirectory admin   442B Aug 13 04:30 apache-tomcat-7.0.64

lrwxr-xr-x   1 mydirectory admin   21B Aug 13 04:30 current -> apache-tomcat-7.0.64/

mydirectory:tomcat mydirectory$

We need to create two instances. However, this is not all, as you can create as many instances as you need.

Begin by creating a new folder, and then give it a name. Inside this folder, create a new one and give it the name *"development."* The following are the Tomcat instances:

```
mydirectory:tomcat mydirectory$ mkdir instances
mydirectory:tomcat mydirectory$ cd instances/
mydirectory:instances        mydirectory$        mkdir
development
mydirectory:instances mydirectory$ ls
total 0
drwxr-xr-x  4 mydirectory  admin   136B Aug 13 04:30
.

drwxr-xr-x  5 mydirectory  admin   170B Aug 13 04:30
..

drwxr-xr-x  2 mydirectory  admin    68B Aug 13 04:30
development

mydirectory:instances mydirectory$ pwd
/usr/local/share/java/tomcat/instances
mydirectory:instances mydirectory$
```

The instances can then be set up as shown below:

```
mydirectory:instances mydirectory$ ls
total 0
drwxr-xr-x  4 mydirectory  admin   136B Aug 13 04:06
.

drwxr-xr-x  5 mydirectory  admin   170B Aug 13 01:56
..

drwxr-xr-x  2 mydirectory  admin    68B Aug 13 04:06
development

drwxr-xr-x  2 mydirectory  admin    68B Aug 13 04:06
production
mydirectory:instances        mydirectory$        cp       -rf
../current/conf/ development/conf

mydirectory:instances        mydirectory$        cp       -rf
../current/logs/ development/logs
```

```
mydirectory:instances    mydirectory$    cp    -rf
../current/temp/ development/temp

mydirectory:instances    mydirectory$    cp    -rf
../current/webapps/ development/webapps

mydirectory:instances    mydirectory$    cp    -rf
../current/work/ development/work

mydirectory:instances mydirectory$ ls development/
total 0
drwxr-xr-x  7 mydirectory  admin   238B Aug 13 04:08
.
drwxr-xr-x  4 mydirectory  admin   136B Aug 13 04:06
..
drwxr-xr-x  9 mydirectory  admin   306B Aug 13 04:07
conf
drwxr-xr-x  2 mydirectory  admin    68B Aug 13 04:07
logs
drwxr-xr-x  3 mydirectory  admin   104B Aug 13 04:08
temp
drwxr-xr-x  7 mydirectory  admin   238B Aug 13 04:08
webapps
drwxr-xr-x  2 mydirectory  admin    68B Aug 13 04:08
work
mydirectory:instances mydirectory$
```

The folders can at this point be removed from the Tomcat installation folder. However, this is not a must.

Home and Base

We need to share the main Tomcat folders. Each of the available instances has a personal folder so that they do not clash with the other instances. Create a *"bin"* folder, and then add the following *"exec.sh"* script to it:

```
#!/bin/bash
TOMCAT_HOME="$(dirname $0)/.."
cd $TOMCAT_HOME && TOMCAT_HOME=$PWD && cd - &> /dev/null

export TOMCAT_HOME

export SK_HOME="$(readlink -f "$TOMCAT_HOME/../../current")"
export SK_BASE="$(readlink -f "$TOMCAT_HOME")"

export SK_OPTS="-Dhttp.port=8080 $SK_OPTS"
export SK_OPTS="-Dhttps.port=8443 $SK_OPTS"
export SK_OPTS="-Dajp.port=8009 $SK_OPTS"
export SK_OPTS="-Dshutdown.port=8005 $SK_OPTS"

echo "JAVA_HOME set to $JAVA_HOME"
echo "SK_BASE set to $SK_BASE"
echo "SK_HOME set to $SK_HOME"

$SK_HOME/bin/"$(basename "$0")" "$@"
```

For MacOS X users, you might be needed to install the *"coreutils"* by use of *"brew,"* and then replace the *"readlink"* with *"greadlink"* for you to achieve the correct behavior.

With the above script, the proper configuration variables will be set up to point to the shared Tomcat and our specific instance folders.

bin/exec.sh

On the bin folder which we created, links to the exec.sh should be created to the following files: sk.sh, startup.sh, shutdown.sh.

The Tomcat Bin scripts are shown below:

```
mydirectory:bin     mydirectory$     ln   -s   exec.sh
catalina.sh
mydirectory:bin mydirectory$ ln -s exec.sh startup.sh
mydirectory:bin     mydirectory$     ln   -s   exec.sh
shutdown.sh
mydirectory:bin mydirectory$ ls
total 32
drwxr-xr-x  6 mydirectory  admin   204B Aug 13 09:14
.
drwxr-xr-x  8 mydirectory  admin   272B Aug 13 07:07
..
lrwxr-xr-x  1 mydirectory  admin      7B Aug 13 10:13
sk.sh -> exec.sh

-rw-r--r--  1 mydirectory  admin   651B Aug 13 07:52
exec.sh
lrwxr-xr-x  1 mydirectory  admin      7B Aug 13 06:24
shutdown.sh -> exec.sh

lrwxr-xr-x  1 mydirectory  admin      7B Aug 13 06:43
startup.sh -> exec.sh
```

mydirectory:bin mydirectory$

With the above script, you will be able to call your original Tomcat, but you will have to call the file *"exec.sh"* first. At this point, the instances should be ready for execution. Just navigate to the development instance folder, and then execute the command *"sh sk.sh run"* or *"sh startup.sh."*

You can duplicate the instance folder for *"development"* to a *"production,"* and then edit the file *"bin/exec.sh"* for it to be updated with the different ports. The property replacement is not executing property for our shutdown port. This is why the file *"conf/server.xml"* has to be edited from the instance of *"production"* and then 80005 replaced with 7005. Once you have fixed this bug, and the property used, you will have not to worry about doing it.

Proper links might have to be established in the files *sk.sh, startup.sh,* and *shutdown.sh* which have been stored in the bin folder. After that, your second instance of the production will be ready to run. For those who are in need of more, the last steps should be repeated while ensuring that the ports that you pick do not conflict with the instances which you have already setup.

At this point, you should be in a position to create new instances without having to make more changes. You may have a single unchanged and untouched instance which can be used for copying from so as to create the others. The Tomcat version should also be updated. This can be done by installing a new distribution and then updating the link to "*current.*" Once the "*jars*" have been placed in the "*libs*" folder of your "*Home*" installation, they will change to become instantly available to the rest of the instances. Instead of having to duplicate your "*conf*" folder, just link it to the one in "*HOME*" and then try to share the configuration between all of the environments. You can also choose to link it between the files which you are in need of sharing. To delete an instance, you just have to delete its "*base*" folder.

Chapter 9- Simplifying Email in an App using Mailgun API

Mailgun is simply an email for developers. It makes use of an elegant mail API for sending and receiving emails for a mobile app. The mailgun plugin has been introduced, and it helps the developers by making the work much easier.

Plugin Installation

The first step should include installing the plugin to a new or an existing app. The following steps are necessary:

1. Inside your app builder, click on *"Create new > From Plugin."* Note that you can create a new app or use an existing one.

2. Under the *"Communication"* category, find the *"Mailgun Mail API."* Check on the plug check box, and then click on the button for *"Import selected plugins."*

3. Open the file for setting by checking the check box on the next page. The start page should also be set to *"mailgun."* Once you are done, click on the button for *"Apply settings."* Addition of the plugin to the app will be done.

Configuration of the Plugin

Now that you have a plugin in your app, you just have to perform a minimal configuration. Let us discuss some of these steps.

Set up of the mailgun Domain

The mailgun domain is used for identifying your account.

1. Begin by signing up for a mailgun account if you don't have one,

2. Open the settings for your domain, and then copy the value of your domain. This should be everything before the ".*mailgun.org.*"

3. The value of the property "*domain*" should then be pasted in the file "*Services/Mailgun_settings.*"

Securing API Credentials

In the Mailgun API, the basic authentication is used for the purpose of authentication. Our aim is to ensure that the authentication information is not kept public on the client part, but it is kept secure on the server. The following steps are necessary to be followed:

1. Click on "*Database*" in the App Builder.

2. Click on *"Create new database."* Give the database a new name.

3. Now click on *"Create new collection."* Give the collection a name.

4. Inside the collection, create two columns.

5. Click on *"+Row"* so as to be able to add data to the collection.

6. In the column for keyName, enter "mailgunAuthProxy."

7. The username and the password can then be encoded. This can be done by opening the Chrome Dev. Tools Console tab and then entering the following and pressing Enter:

>window.btoa("api:key-0ce1xxxxxx");

Conclusion

It can be concluded that DevOps is a culture which is employed in organizations. In this case, the software development team works closely and in harmony with the IT professionals of the company so as to deliver software o the organization. When employed in any organization, the process of software development, right from the planning stage to the deployment stage will be made quick, easy, and highly reliable.

It is an aim of each and every organization to improve on the performance of their teams. However, just talking about it will not help. We have to implement a culture in the team. Targets should be set up, and these will act as a measure for us to know how a particular team is doing or progressing. Once the target has been set, there will also be a smooth moving or correlation between members of the development team. They will also be very focused on achieving that. The managers will also have the right data for the purpose of decision-making. They will also be in a position to assess the viability of the decisions they make based on the outcome that they get.

The metrics which can be used for evaluating the performance of DevOp teams have been discussed. If these are used and something negative about the organization is found, then try to do away with it. There are numerous DevOp operations which we could have discussed in this book. However, the ones discussed here should help you in gaining an insight into how to implement DevOps.

www.ingramcontent.com/pod-product-compliance
Lightning Source LLC
Chambersburg PA
CBHW070857070326
40690CB00009B/1884